Essential Question
How do people work with animals?

TEACH A DOG!

by Justin Yong

Dogs like to play!

Dogs are good pets!
Would you like to teach
a dog? It's hard work,
but it's fun.

Give a dog a treat when he behaves.

Then say, "Good dog!"

This dog wants the treat.

The girl pets her dog when it sits.

First, teach the dog the word *sit*.

If she sits, give her a treat.

Next, put out your hand and say, "Stay!"

If she stays, give her a treat.

Now say, "Come!" If she is clever, she will come!

This dog learns to stay.

This dog is shy or scared.

This dog sits up to beg.

A dog can't talk. So he gives a signal. If his tail is down, he's sad.

This dog wants to play.

If he's wagging his tail, he's happy.

If he's digging, maybe he found a bone!

These dogs learn to walk on a leash.

Walk a dog! First, put on the leash. Walk slowly and keep the dog near you.

Stop walking if the dog pulls. Wait for her to be still.

This dog is pulling on the leash.

Exercise helps keep a dog healthy.

You can run with a dog. But slow down if the dog pants too much.

Write down the rules.
Then help a friend
teach a dog!

Writing down the
rules will help you
remember them.

Respond to Reading

Retell

Use your own words to retell *Teach a Dog!* in order.

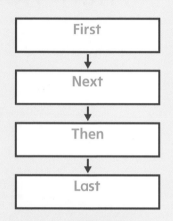

First

↓

Next

↓

Then

↓

Last

Text Evidence

1. Look at page 5. What do you teach a dog after "stay"? Sequence

2. Look at page 8. What do you do before you walk a dog?

   Sequence

3. How do you know that *Teach a Dog!* is nonfiction? Genre

Genre Nonfiction

Compare Texts
Read about how animals work
with people.

Working with Dolphins

Dolphins can be trained.

Dolphins are good helpers! They can help people who are sick or hurt.

The woman in the photo teaches dolphins. She shows them how to work with children. Dolphins like kids!

Some trainers
give dolphins
fish as a treat.

Dolphins also do tricks.
A dolphin can stand up
or jump! Dolphins make
people happy.

Make Connections
Look at both stories. How do
people teach animals? Text to Text

Focus on
Social Studies

Purpose To find out which pet students like best

What to Do

Step 1 ▶ Ask classmates, "Which pet do you like best?"

Step 2 ▶ Write the answers. Count how many classmates like each kind of pet on your list.

Step 3 ▶ Share the answers with the class.